Sing the Christmas Story

A carol service for schools and churches

Val Hawthorne

kevin mayhew

kevin mayhew

First published in Great Britain in 2005 by Kevin Mayhew Ltd
Buxhall, Stowmarket, Suffolk IP14 3BW
Tel: +44 (0) 1449 737978 Fax: +44 (0) 1449 737834
E-mail: info@kevinmayhewltd.com

www.kevinmayhew.com

9 8 7 6 5 4 3 2

ISBN 978 1 84417 444 7
ISMN M 57024 480 5
Catalogue No. 1450345

Cover design: Sara-Jane Came
Cover illustration © copyright Joto24. Agency: Dreamstime.com
Music setting: Barry Hart and Donald Thomson
Proof reading: Marian Hellen

Printed and bound in Great Britain

Contents

Numbers in brackets are for the backing track

A note about copyright in musicals

Copyright has existed for hundreds of years as a means of protecting the worth of a piece of music or text. It provides income for the composer and publisher and helps to keep the works available in print at an affordable price.

Performance Licence

Any public performance of a piece of copyright music requires a licence. Music remains protected by copyright for 70 years after the death of the composer.

Even if you do not intend to charge an entrance fee for your performance, it is necessary to apply for a licence and the minimum fee will still be payable. If you are staging more than one performance without an admission charge, you need only pay the minimum licence fee once.

If you are charging for admission, the Performance Licence will cost 10% of gross ticket sales, plus VAT, subject to the minimum fee.

The only time a performing fee is not payable is when the musical is performed within a worship service and forms part of the act of worship.

Photocopying Licence

The words and music of the songs in our musicals are protected by copyright and may not be photocopied without permission. The music may not be photocopied at all – users are expected to purchase enough copies for those performers who require the full music. The texts may be copied for learning purposes only, provided that:

• The following acknowledgement is included on each copy: © Kevin Mayhew Ltd. Used by permission from *name of musical*. Licence number......

• You pay a copyright fee of £10.00 (inc. VAT), which should be added to your performance licence cheque (payable to Kevin Mayhew Ltd).

• All copies are destroyed after use.

Please note that the music and texts of our musicals are not covered by a CCL licence.

Duplicating CDs

Unfortunately we are unable to give permission for copying the accompanying CDs. It is illegal to duplicate any copyright sound recording, even for home use.

If you have any queries about copyright in Kevin Mayhew publications, please call our Copyright Department on 01449 737978.

There is a photocopiable licence application form at the back of our musicals.

Foreword

This carol service is intended for use in schools at KS2 and as a family service in churches. The songs for a children's choir tell the Christmas story, from the prophecies to the visit of the wise men. The final song reminds us that the message of Christmas is not just once a year but for always.

The Bible readings use the *Good News* version. The sentences preceding the songs could be spoken by a member of the choir.

The carols for everyone do not include all possible verses but those suitable for a primarily children's service.

I have suggested a place for prayers to be inserted as appropriate for individual situations.

The format lends itself to including tableaux or simple mime to illustrate the readings and songs.

My thanks to the choir of Walter Halls Primary School in Nottingham and their teacher Lynne Murphy for working so hard and for singing the songs so beautifully in 2003.

VAL HAWTHORNE

SING THE CHRISTMAS STORY

A Carol Service for Schools and Churches
Devised with original songs by Val Hawthorne

1. COME WITH US

Let us go to Bethlehem and see this thing that has happened which the Lord has made known unto us.

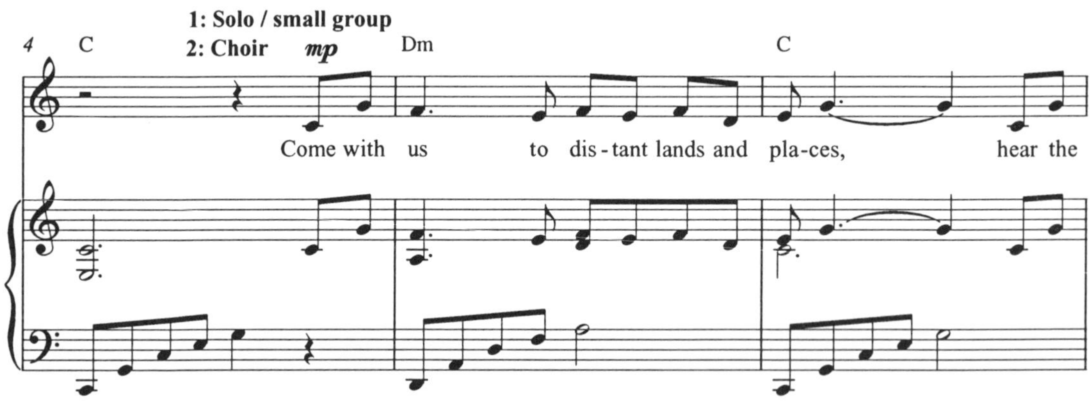

6

10
Am
Dm
G
fa - ces
of those
whose sto - ry we all know.
Come with
13
Dm
C
Dm
us
and hear the an-gels sing-ing,
see the star
and find the sta-ble
16
Em
F
Am
bare.
Look in - side
and as the bells are ring-ing,
19
rit.
Dm
F/G
G
p
1.
C
2.
C
you may find your trea - sure
there.
there.
rit.
p

2. DING DONG, MERRILY ON HIGH!

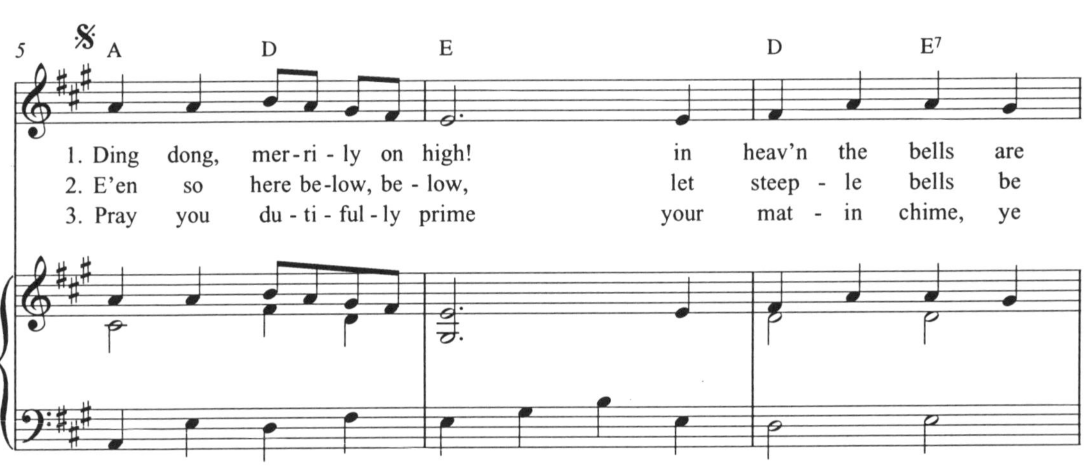

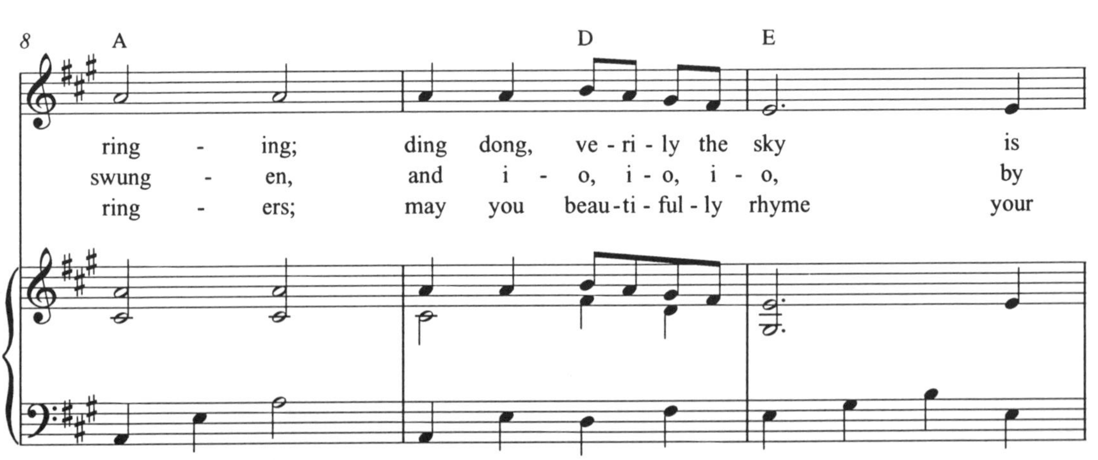

8

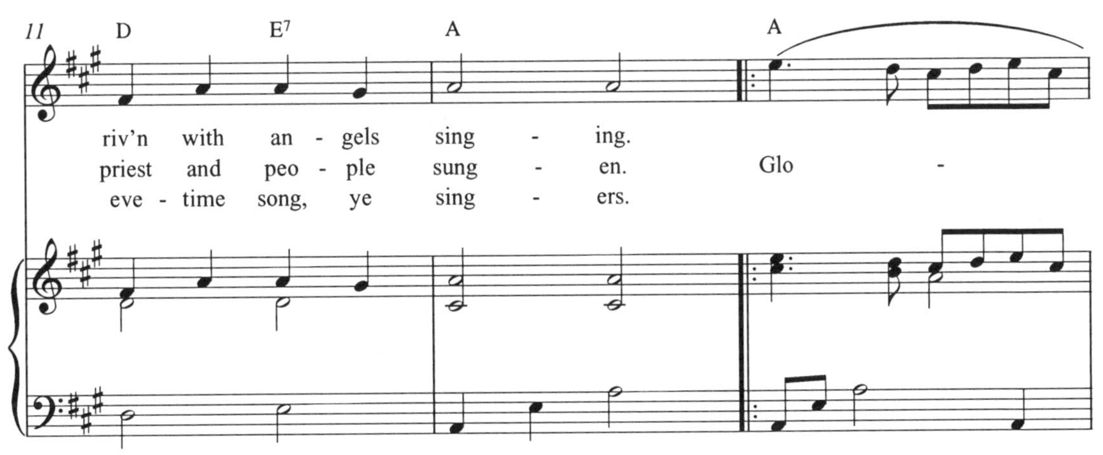

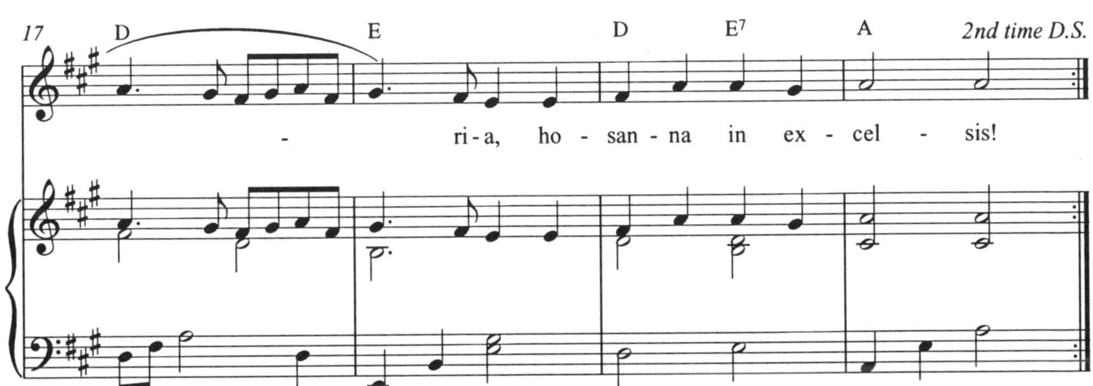

Text: George Ratcliffe Woodward (1848-1934)
Music: Traditional French melody arr. Val Hawthorne

9

3. GOD'S WORLD

In the beginning God created the world
and God saw all that he had made and it was very good.

9
D
G6
God had made it all and he made it real - ly good, but the
God has made a pro - mise and he made it real - ly good, but the
11
A
D
peo - ple who lived in it — they ne - ver un - der - stood.
peo - ple would - n't lis - ten and they ne - ver un - der - stood.
13
G
F#m
Em7
D
Ev - 'ry-thing went wrong time and time a - gain,
Now the time is here when the words come true,
15
G
A
D
A7
D
ev - en though God had made the way plain.
there is a chance for mak - ing things new.

17
G   F#m   Em7   D
Now there is a se - cond chance, he does - n't let you down.
God has kept his pro - mise and he does - n't let you down.

19
E7   A
Bet - ter keep an eye on Beth - le - hem town.
Bet - ter take a look in Beth - le - hem town.

21
D   G6
God has made a world and he wants it to be good, but the
God so loved the world he sent a mes - sage that is new for the

1.
23
A   D
peo - ple who live in it have ne - ver un - der-stood.

4. READING: The Prophets foretell the birth of a Saviour
Isaiah 9:2, 6, 7a; Micah 5:2

The people who walked in darkness have seen a great light. They lived in a land of shadows, but now the light is shining on them. A child is born to us! A son is given to us! And he will be our ruler. He will be called, 'Wonderful Counsellor, Mighty God, Eternal Father, Prince of Peace.' His royal power will continue to grow; his kingdom will always be at peace.

The Lord says 'Bethlehem Ephrathah, you are one of the smallest towns in Judah but out of you I will bring a ruler for Israel, whose family line goes back to ancient times.'

5. ONCE IN ROYAL DAVID'S CITY

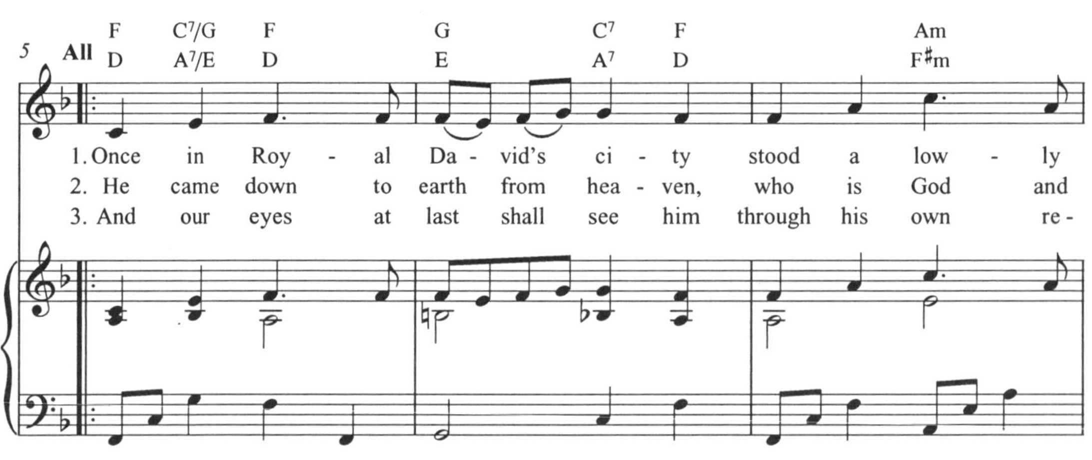

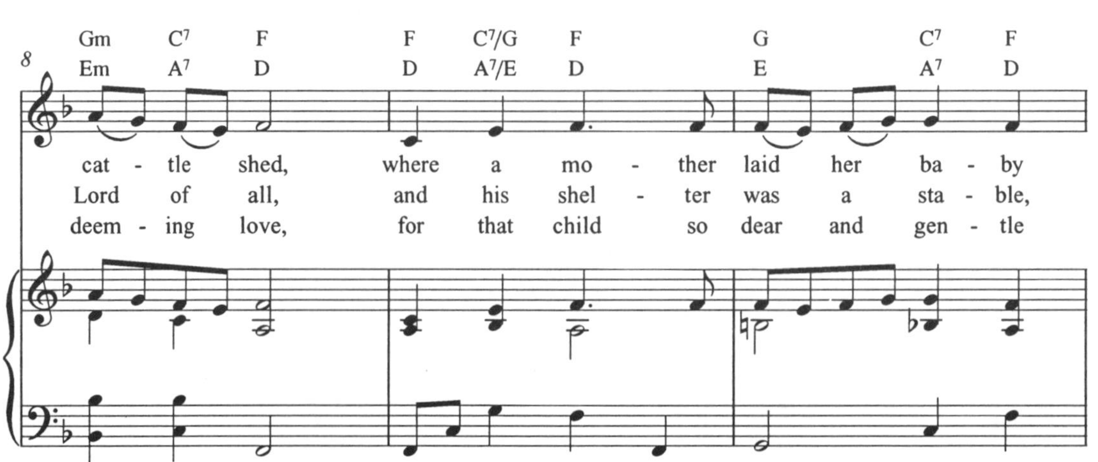

Text: Cecil Frances Alexander (1818-1895)
Music: Henry John Gauntlett (1805-1876) arr. Val Hawthorne

6. READING: The angel visits Mary
Luke 1:26-33

In the sixth month God sent the angel Gabriel to a town in Galilee named Nazareth. He had a message for a young woman promised in marriage to a man named Joseph, who was a descendant of King David. Her name was Mary. The angel came to her and said, 'Peace be with you. The Lord is with you and has greatly blessed you.'

Mary was deeply troubled by the angel's message and she wondered what his words meant. The angel said to her, 'Don't be afraid Mary; God has been gracious to you. You will become pregnant and give birth to a son, and you will name him Jesus. He will be great and will be called the Son of the Most High God. The Lord God will make him a king of the descendants of Jacob for ever; his kingdom will never end.'

7. MARY AND THE ANGEL

The angel said 'Do not be afraid, Mary. You have found favour with God.'

8. READING: The decree is issued

Luke 2:1-3

At that time the Emperor Augustus ordered a census to be taken throughout the Roman Empire. When the first census took place Quirinius was the governor of Syria. Everyone then went to register himself, each to his own town.

9. O LITTLE TOWN OF BETHLEHEM

Text: Phillips Brooks (1835-1893) alt.
Music: Traditional English melody collected by
Ralph Vaughan Williams (1872-1958) arr. Val Hawthorne

10. READING: Mary and Joseph travel to Bethlehem

Luke 2:4-5

Joseph went from the town of Nazareth in Galilee to the town of Bethlehem in Judea, the birthplace of King David. Joseph went there because he was a descendant of David. He went to register with Mary, who was promised in marriage to him.

11. NO ROOM

There was no room for them in the inn.

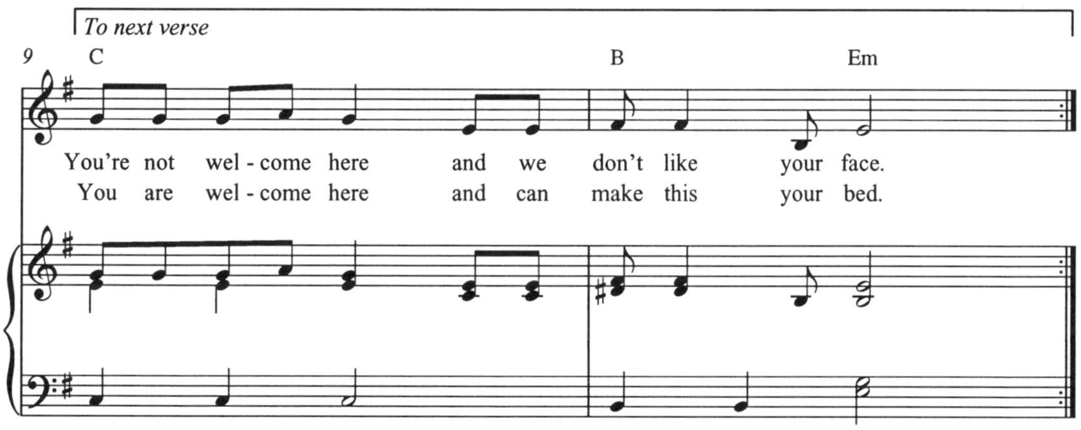

12. READING: Mary gives birth to her son
Luke 2:6-7

While they were in Bethlehem the time came for Mary to have her baby. She gave birth to her first-born son, wrapped him in cloths and laid him in the manger because there was no room for them to stay in the inn.

13. ALLELUIA ROUND

Unto us a child is born.

Flowing ($\text{♩.} = 60$)

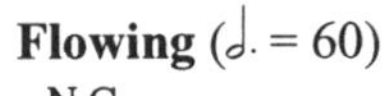

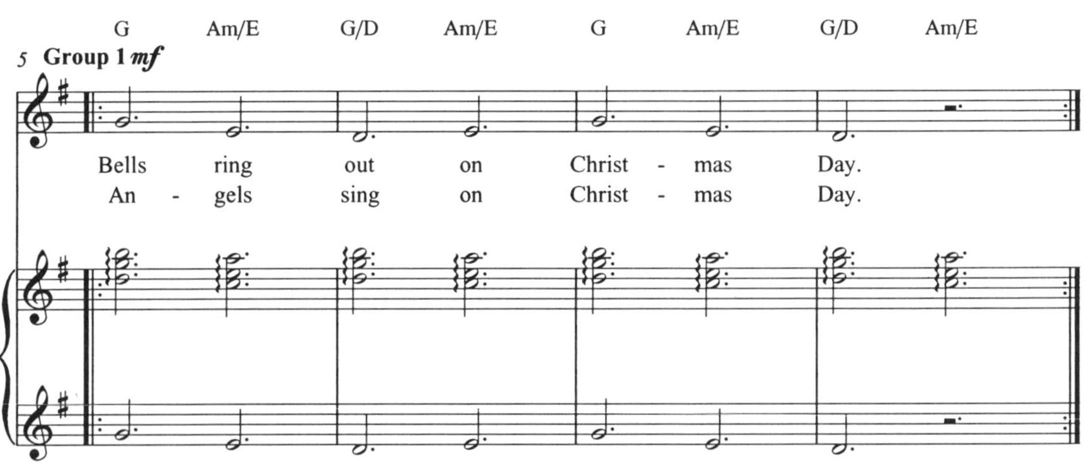

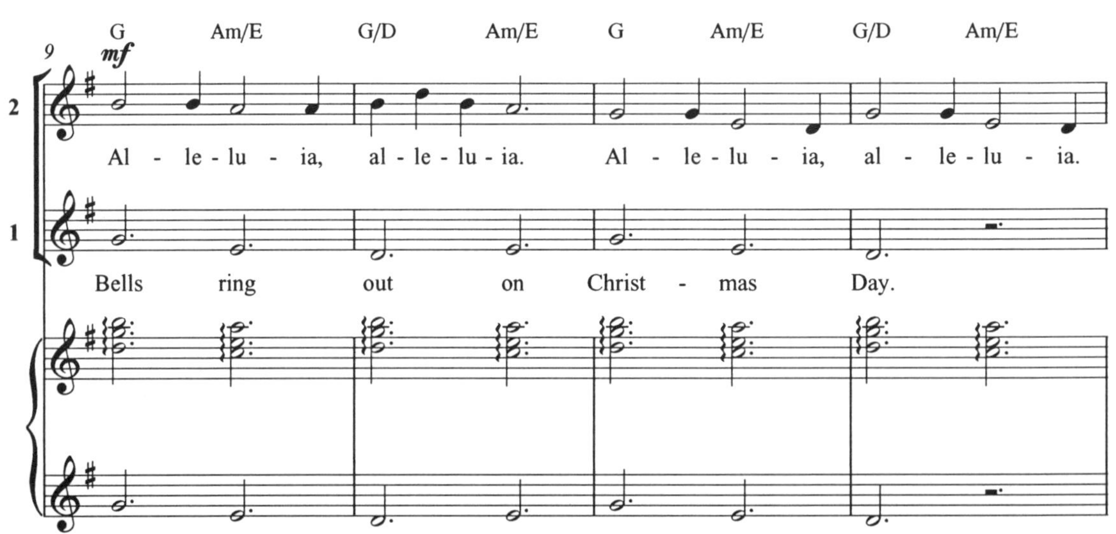

13
G Am/E G/D Am/E G Am/E G/D Am/E
Al - le - lu - ia, al - le - lu - ia. Al - le - lu - ia.
An - gels sing on Christ - mas Day.

17
mf
3
G Am/E G/D Am/E G Am/E G/D Am/E
Come to Beth - le-hem, Je - sus is born, Je - sus is born.
2
Al - le - lu - ia, al - le - lu - ia. Al - le - lu - ia, al - le - lu - ia.
1
Bells ring out on Christ - mas Day.

21
G Am/E G/D Am/E G Am/E G/D Am/E
Come to Beth - le-hem, Je - sus is born to - day.
Al - le - lu - ia, al - le - lu - ia. Al - le - lu - ia.
An - gels sing on Christ - mas Day.

G Am/E G/D Am/E G Am/E G/D Am/E
25
mf
Peace on earth, good news we bring.
Come to Beth - le-hem, Je - sus is born, Je - sus is born.
Al - le -lu - ia, al - le -lu - ia. Al - le -lu - ia, al - le -lu - ia.
Bells ring out on Christ - mas Day.
29
G G/D Am/E G Am/E G/D Am/E G/D
1. 2.
Prai - ses sing to heav - en's King. King.
Come to Beth - le-hem, Je - sus is born to - day. day.
Al - le -lu - ia, al - le -lu - ia. Al - le -lu - ia. ia.
An - gels sing on Christ - mas Day. Day.
1. 2.

14. SILENT NIGHT

Text: Joseph Mohr (1792-1848) trans. John Freeman Young (1820-1885)
Music: Franz Grüber (1787-1863) arr. Val Hawthorne

15. READING: The shepherds hear the news

Luke 2:8-14

There were some shepherds in that part of the country who were spending the night in the fields, taking care of their flocks. An angel of the Lord appeared to them, and the glory of the Lord shone over them. They were terribly afraid, but the angel said to them, 'Don't be afraid! I am here with good news for you, which will bring great joy to all the people. This very day, in David's town, your Saviour was born – Christ the Lord! And this is what will prove it to you; you will find a baby wrapped in strips of cloth and lying in a manger.'

Suddenly a great army of heaven's angels appeared with the angel, singing praises to God: 'Glory to God in the highest heaven, and peace on earth to those with whom he is pleased!'

16. THE ANGELS WAKE THE SHEPHERDS

The angel said, 'Do not be afraid. I bring you good news.'

peo - ple have been wait - ing in dark - ness for too long.
Don't wait for the morn - ing but hur - ry on your way.
On this day a child is born and he's a Sa - viour king.
In the ci - ty down be - low you'll find the in - fant King.
This is the song we sing:
This is the news we bring:
Glo - ry be to
God, glo - ry be to God, peace to all the folk on

31
Am C⁷sus⁴ C⁷ F⁶ F
F♯m A⁷sus⁴ A⁷ D⁶ D
earth. Glo - ry be to God,

35
Gm F Gm
Em D Em
glo - ry be to God, hear a-bout a Sa - viour's

1.
B♭ F F⁶ Dm
G D D⁶ Bm
birth.
mf

2.
43
Gm C⁷ B♭ F
Em A⁷ G rit. D
birth.
rit.

17. READING: The shepherds go to Bethlehem
Luke 2:15-20

When the angels went away from them back to heaven, the shepherds said one to another, 'Let's go to Bethlehem and see this thing that has happened, which the Lord has told us.'

So they hurried off and found Mary and Joseph and saw the baby lying in a manger. When the shepherds saw him they told them what the angel had said about the child. And all who heard it were amazed at what the shepherds said.

Mary remembered all these things and thought deeply about them. The shepherds went back, singing praises to God for all they had heard and seen; it was just as the angel told them.

18. IN THE BLEAK MIDWINTER

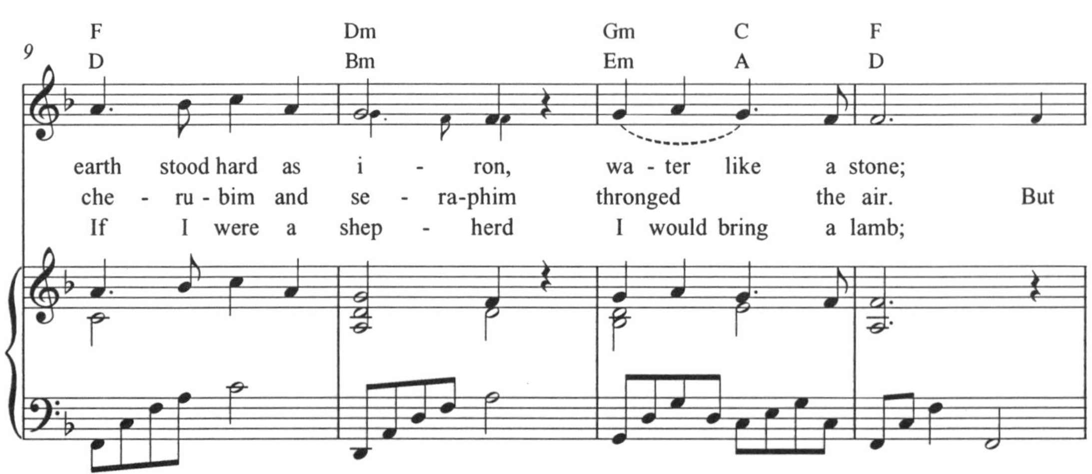

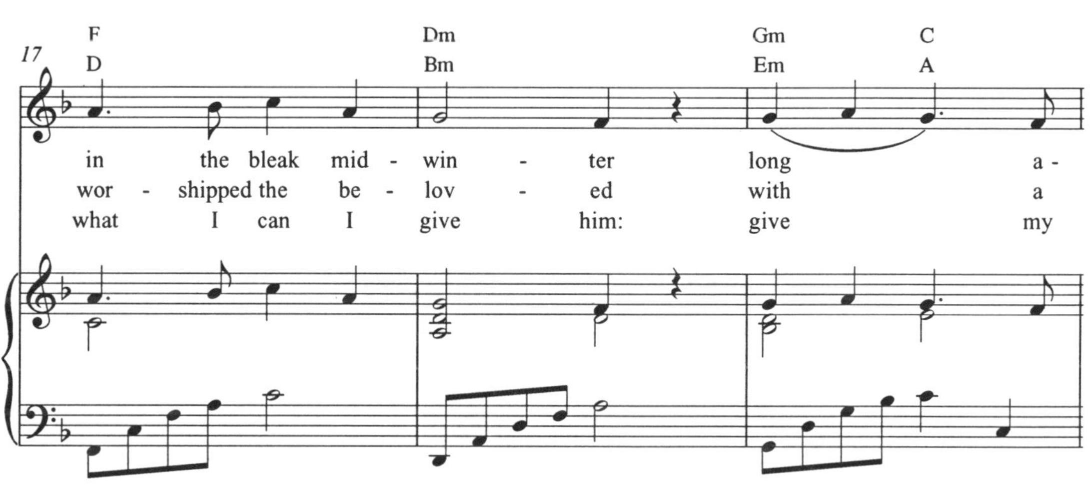

Text: Christina Georgina Rossetti (1830-1894)
Music: Gustav Holst (1874-1934) arr. Val Hawthorne

19. READING: The Wise Men follow the star
Matthew 2:1-5a, 7, 8

Jesus was born in the town of Bethlehem in Judea, during the time when Herod was king. Soon afterwards some men who studied the stars came from the east to Jerusalem and asked, 'Where is the baby born to be the king of the Jews? We saw his star when it came up in the east, and we have come to worship him.'

When King Herod heard about this he was very upset, and so was everyone else in Jerusalem. He called together all the chief priests and the teachers of the Law and asked them, 'Where will the Messiah be born?'

'In the town of Bethlehem in Judea,' they answered . . .

So Herod called the visitors from the east to a secret meeting and found out from them the exact time the star had appeared. Then he sent them to Bethlehem with these instructions: 'Go and make a careful search for the child, and when you find him, let me know, so that I too may worship him.'

20. THE WISE MEN REMEMBER

We have seen his star in the east and have come to worship him.

10
Gm
A
3rd time to CODA

fall?
fall?
fall.

So far a - way,
So far a - way,
There in that place,

so long a - go,
so long a - go,
we saw his face,

what did we
what did we
un - der-stood

A little quicker and brighter (♩. = 84)

12
poco rit.
D
G⁶
mf

know?
know?

The
At

jour-ney was of-ten a sham-bles,
last we were at He-rod's court,

we'd

poco rit.

mf

14
Em⁷
F♯m
Bm
Em⁷

end - less o - ver-night ram-bles,
heard that we had to re - port.

tra - vel-ling on to a place we'd no id-ea
We shook in our shoes; he seemed so ang-ry and

16
Em⁷/A
A
D
G⁶

where.
wild.

The ser-vants be - gan to com-plain,
His men all took one look at us

we were
and

18
Em7   F#m   Bm   E
rall.
lost in the de - sert a - gain   and ma - ny a time we all felt close to des-
then threw the whole book at us,   but to our sur - prise said they want-ed to vi - sit the
rall.

Tempo I   CODA
20
A   N.C.   Asus4   A   N.C.
p
pair.   2. Do you re -   why.   (Hum)
child.   3. Now I re -
p

Dm   Gm   rit.
22
rit.

Dm   Gm   A   Dm
p
24
p
8vb

21. READING: The Wise Men find Jesus

Matthew 2:9-11

And so they left, and on their way they saw the same star they had seen in the east. When they saw it, how happy they were, what joy was theirs! It went ahead of them until it stopped over the place where the child was. They went into the house, and when they saw the child with his mother Mary, they knelt down and worshipped him. They brought out their gifts of gold, frankincense and myrrh, and presented them to him.

22. A SONG OF CHRISTMAS

God so loved the world he gave his only Son.

Moving along ($\bullet. = 80$)

Optional tuned percussion plays R.H. chords

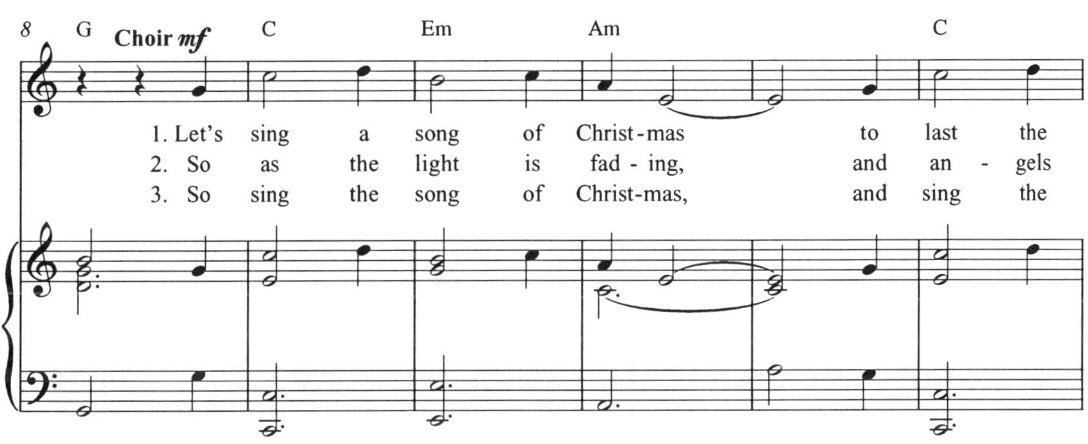

20 Am   Dm   G   C
world,   of pro - mis - es all   come   true.   And   as   the
sky   and morn - ing is draw - ing near.   We   can - not
world,   of pro - mi - ses all   come   true.   So   join the

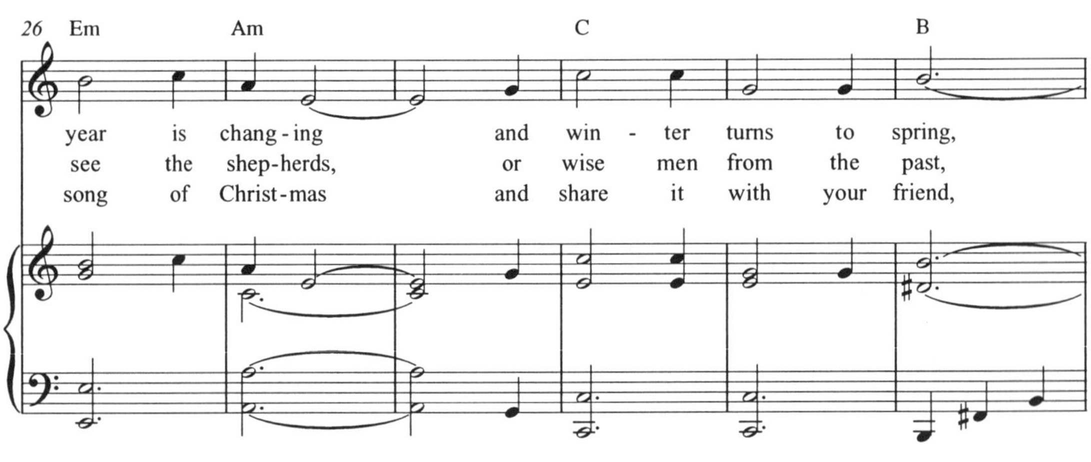

26 Em   Am   C   B
year   is   chang - ing   and   win - ter turns   to   spring,
see   the shep - herds,   or   wise men   from   the past,
song   of   Christ - mas   and   share it   with   your friend,

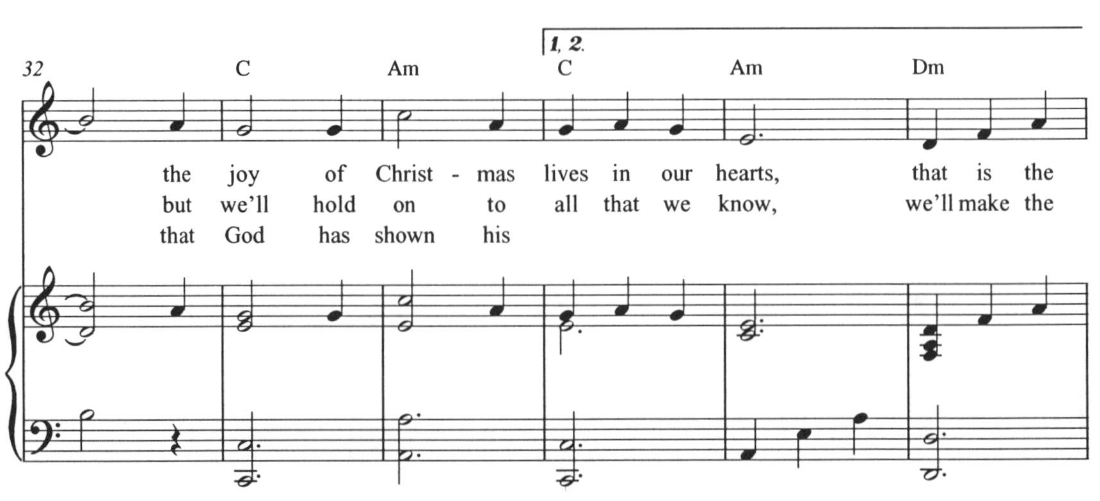

1, 2.
32   C   Am   C   Am   Dm
the joy   of Christ - mas lives in our hearts,   that is the
but we'll hold on   to   all that we know,   we'll make the
that God has shown his

song we sing.
pro - mise last.
love for us all,
love that will ne - ver end.
Ne - ver end. end.

23. PRAYERS

24. O COME, ALL YE FAITHFUL

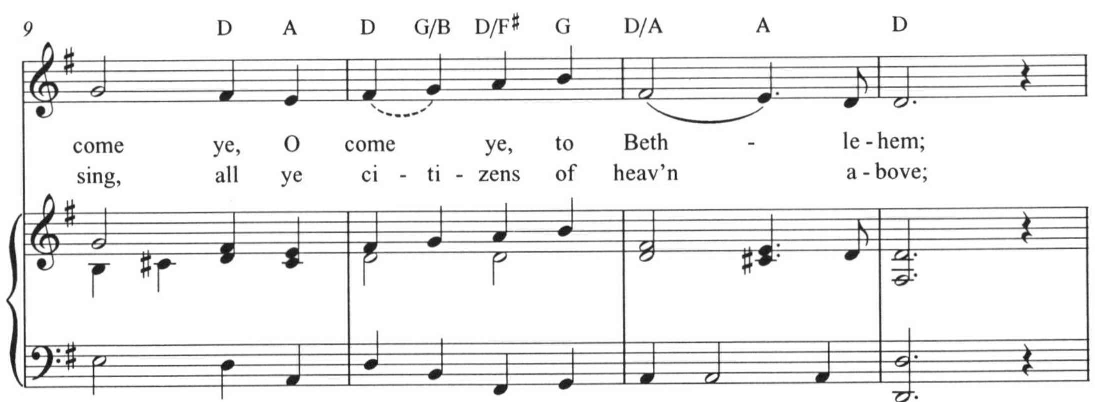

Text: Original Latin attributed to John Francis Wade (1711-1786)
trans. Frederick Oakeley (1802-1880)
Music: Attributed to John Francis Wade (1711-1786)
arr. Val Hawthorne

25. FINAL PRAYER OF BLESSING

SING THE CHRISTMAS STORY

Val Hawthorne

1. COME WITH US

Come with us to distant lands and places,
hear the words of prophets long a-go.
Watch with us and you may see the faces
of those whose story we all know.
Come with us and hear the angels singing,
see the star and find the stable bare.
Look inside and as the bells are ringing,
you may find your treasure there.

2. DING DONG, MERRILY ON HIGH!

1. Ding dong, merrily on high!
   in heav'n the bells are ringing;
   ding dong, verily the sky
   is riv'n with angels singing.
   Gloria, hosanna in excelsis!

2. E'en so here below, below,
   let steeple bells be swungen,
   and io, io, io,
   by priest and people sungen.
   Gloria, hosanna in excelsis!

3. Pray you dutifully prime
   your matin chime, ye ringers;
   may you beautifully rhyme
   your evetime song, ye singers.
   Gloria, hosanna in excelsis!

3. GOD'S WORLD

1. Many years ago when the
   world had just begun,
   everything was beautiful
   underneath the sun.
   God had made it all
   and he made it really good,
   but the people who lived in it –
   they never understood.
   Everything went wrong
   time and time again,
   even though God
   had made the way plain.
   Now there is a second chance,
   he doesn't let you down.
   Better keep an eye
   on Bethlehem town.
   God has made a world
   and he wants it to be good,
   but the people who live in it
   have never understood.

2. Many prophets told them
   all the way it had to be,
   written in the Book it's there
   for everyone to see.
   God has made a promise
   and he made it really good,
   but the people wouldn't listen
   and they never understood.
   Now the time is here
   when the words come true,
   there is a chance for making things new.
   God has kept his promise
   and he doesn't let you down.
   Better take a look in Bethlehem town.
   God so loved the world
   he sent a message that is new
   for the people who live in it –
   and that's you!

5. ONCE IN ROYAL DAVID'S CITY

1. Once in Royal David's city
   stood a lowly cattle shed,
   where a mother laid her baby
   in a manger for his bed:
   Mary was that mother mild,
   Jesus Christ her little child.

2. He came down to earth from heaven,
   who is God and Lord of all,
   and his shelter was a stable,
   and his cradle was a stall;
   with the poor and mean and lowly
   lived on earth our Saviour holy.

3. And our eyes at last shall see him
   through his own redeeming love,
   for that child so dear and gentle
   is our Lord in heav'n above;
   and he leads his children on
   to the place where he is gone.

7. MARY AND THE ANGEL

1. Very early in the morning,
   softly at the break of day,
   Mary sits dreaming, then she looks
   and sees there's an angel,
   and hears him say:
   'Ma-ry lis-ten, you're the one.
   God chose you to be
   the mother here of his son.'

2. Mary bows her head in worship
   as she wonders at this birth.
   'How can this be that God has chosen
   me for this purpose,
   down here on earth?'
   'Mary listen, only trust.
   This child is to show to all the world
   God is with us. God is with us.'

9. O LITTLE TOWN OF BETHLEHEM

1. O little town of Bethlehem,
   how still we see thee lie!
   Above thy deep and dreamless sleep
   the silent stars go by.
   Yet in thy dark streets shineth
   the everlasting light;
   the hopes and fears of all the years
   are met in thee tonight.

2. How silently, how silently
   the wondrous gift is giv'n!
   So God imparts to human hearts
   the blessings of his heav'n.
   No ear may hear his coming;
   but in this world of sin,
   where meek souls will receive him,
   still the dear Christ enters in.

3. O holy child of Bethlehem,
   descend to us, we pray;
   cast out our sin, and enter in,
   be born in us today.
   We hear the Christmas angels
   the great glad tidings tell:
   O come to us, abide with us,
   our Lord Emmanuel.

11. NO ROOM

1. There is no room, no room in the inn
   for those who are strangers
   new to this place.
   There's no use in waiting,
   standing in the rain.
   You're not welcome here and we
   don't like your face.

2. There is no room, no room in the inn,
   but if you don't mind
   there is a cattle shed.
   Don't stand out there waiting,
   come in from the rain.
   You are welcome here and can
   make this your bed.

3. Is there no room, no room for the lonely?
   Those who are cold
   with nowhere to stay?
   Must they keep on waiting,
   standing in the rain?
   Are they welcome here
   on this Christmas Day?

13. ALLELUIA ROUND

Bells ring out on Christmas Day.
Angels sing on Christmas Day.

Alleluia, alleluia. Alleluia, alleluia.
Alleluia, alleluia. Alleluia.

Come to Bethlehem, Jesus is born,
Jesus is born.
Come to Bethlehem, Jesus is born today.

Peace on earth, good news we bring.
Praises sing to heaven's King.

14. SILENT NIGHT

1. Silent night, holy night.
   All is calm, all is bright,
   round yon virgin mother and child;
   holy infant so tender and mild,
   sleep in heavenly peace,
   sleep in heavenly peace.

2. Silent night, holy night.
   Shepherds quake at the sight,
   glories stream from heaven afar,
   heav'nly host sing alleluia:
   Christ the Saviour is born,
   Christ the Saviour is born.

16. THE ANGELS WAKE THE SHEPHERDS

1. Shepherds come and wake now
   and listen to this song,
   people have been waiting
   in darkness for too long.
   On this day a child is born

and he's a Saviour king.
This is the song we sing:

*Glory be to God, glory be to God,
peace to all the folk on earth.
Glory be to God, glory be to God,
hear about a Saviour's birth.*

2. Shepherds rise and go now,
   get up and don't delay.
   Don't wait for the morning
   but hurry on your way.
   In the city down below
   you'll find the infant King.
   This is the news we bring:

Refrain

18. IN THE BLEAK MIDWINTER

1. In the bleak midwinter
      frosty wind made moan,
   earth stood hard as iron,
      water like a stone;
   snow had fallen, snow on snow,
      snow on snow,
   in the bleak midwinter long ago.

2. Angels and archangels
      may have gathered there,
   cherubim and seraphim
      thronged the air.
   But only his mother in her maiden bliss
   worshipped the beloved with a kiss.

3. What can I give him,
      poor as I am?
   If I were a shepherd
      I would bring a lamb;
   if I were a wise man I would do my part,
   yet what I can I give him: give my heart.

20. THE WISE MEN REMEMBER

1. Do you remember? Do you recall?
   The night we saw the star,
   the brightest star by far?
   Was it December or was it the fall?
   So far away, so long ago,
   what did we know?
   The journey was often a shambles,
   endless overnight rambles,
   travelling on to a place
   we'd no idea where.
   The servants began to complain,
   we were lost in the desert again
   and many a time
   we all felt close to despair.

2. Do you remember? Do you recall?
   The night we followed the star,
   the brightest star by far?
   Was it December or was it the fall?
   So far away, so long ago,
   what did we know?
   At last we were at Herod's court,
   we'd heard that we had to report.
   We shook in our shoes;
   he seemed so angry and wild.
   His men all took one look at us
   and then threw the whole book at us,
   but to our surprise
   said they wanted to visit the child.

3. Now I remember, now I recall
   the night the star on high
   shone brighter in the sky.
   It was December or maybe the fall.
   There in that place, we saw his face,
   understood why.

22. A SONG OF CHRISTMAS

1. Let's sing a song of Christmas
   to last the whole year through.
   A song of love to fill the whole world,
   of promises all come true.
   And as the year is changing

and winter turns to spring,
the joy of Christmas lives in our hearts,
that is the song we sing.

2. So as the light is fading,
   and angels disappear,
   the star no longer shines in the sky
   and morning is drawing near.
   We cannot see the shepherds,
   or wise men from the past,
   but we'll hold on to all that we know,
   we'll make the promise last.

3. So sing the song of Christmas,
   and sing the whole year through
   a song of peace to fill the whole world,
   of promises all come true.
   So join the song of Christmas
   and share it with your friend,
   that God has shown his love for us all,
   love that will never end.

24. O COME, ALL YE FAITHFUL

1. O come, all ye faithful,
   joyful and triumphant,
   O come ye, O come ye, to Bethlehem;
   come and behold him,
   born the king of angels:

   O come, let us adore him,
   O come, let us adore him,
   O come, let us adore him,
   Christ the Lord.

2. Sing, choirs of angels,
   sing in exultation,
   sing, all ye citizens of heav'n above;
   glory to God in the highest:

Refrain

KEVIN MAYHEW PERFORMANCE AND PHOTOCOPYING LICENCE FORM

We are delighted that you are considering *Sing the Christmas Story* for production.
Please note that a performance licence is required and royalties are payable as follows:

10% of gross takings, plus VAT
(Minimum fee: £22.00 + VAT = £25.85)

This fee is valid until 31 December 2008. After that date, please contact the Copyright Department for information.

This form should be returned to the Copyright Department at Kevin Mayhew Ltd. A copy, including our performance licence number, will be returned to you.

Name of Organisation ____

Contact name ____

Contact address ____

____

Postcode ____

Contact Telephone No. ________________________ **Contact Fax No.** _______________

E-mail ____

Date(s) of performance(s) ____

Venue ____

Seating capacity ____

Proposed ticket price ____

Please tick:

☐ I am not charging admission for my performance.
I enclose the minimum fee.

☐ I am charging admission and undertake to submit performance fees due to Kevin Mayhew Ltd. within 28 days of the last performance, together with a statement of gross takings.

☐ I require a words-only photocopying licence and enclose £10.00 (inc. VAT).

Signature ____

Name (please print) ____

On behalf of ____

Address if different from above ____

____

- -

To be completed by Kevin Mayhew Copyright Department:

Performance/Photocopying Licence No _______________________________________

is issued to _______________________________ For _____________ performance(s)

of _______________________________ on _______________________________

Signed _______________________________ for Kevin Mayhew Ltd.   Date _______________

Copyright Department, Kevin Mayhew Ltd, Buxhall, Stowmarket, Suffolk, IP14 3BW
Telephone number: UK 01449 737978   International +44 1449 737978
Fax number: UK 01449 737834   International +44 1449 737834
E-mail: copyright@kevinmayhewltd.com